The
ENNEAGRAM
of BELONGING
WORKBOOK

The ENNEAGRAM *of* BELONGING WORKBOOK

Mapping Your Unique Path
to Self-Acceptance

CHRISTOPHER L. HEUERTZ
with ESTEE ZANDEE

ZONDERVAN THRIVE

The Enneagram of Belonging Workbook
Copyright © 2020 by Christopher L. Heuertz

Requests for information should be addressed to:
Zondervan, *3900 Sparks Dr. SE, Grand Rapids, Michigan 49546*

Zondervan titles may be purchased in bulk for educational, business, fundraising, or sales promotional use. For information, please email SpecialMarkets@Zondervan.com.

ISBN 978-0-310-35944-9 (softcover)

ISBN 978-0-310-35945-6 (ebook)

Author is represented by The Christopher Ferebee Agency, www.christopherferebee.com.

Zondervan Thrive, an imprint of Zondervan, publishes books that empower readers with insightful, expert-driven ideas for a life of thriving in today's world.

Author photo: PS Drickey
Cover and interior illustrations: Elnora Turner
Interior design: Kait Lamphere

Printed in the United States of America

20 21 22 23 24 25 26 27 28 29 30 31 32 33 /LSC/ 15 14 13 12 11 10 9 8 7 6 5 4 3 2 1

Contents

Introduction 7

Session 1: *The Path to Belonging (Chapter 1)* 11
    Belong → Behave → Believe → Become
    Enneagram Overview
    Intelligence Centers

Session 2: *Beyond Type (Chapters 2–5)* 23
    Redefining Type and the Childhood Wounds
    Wings
    Integration and Disintegration

Session 3: *Belonging for the Mind (Chapters 6–7)* 49
    Holy Ideas
    Fixations

Session 4: *Belonging for the Heart (Chapters 8–9)* 73
    Virtues
    Passions

Session 5: *Belonging for the Body (Chapter 10)* 89
    Instincts and Subtypes

Conclusion 105
Enneagram Consultations and Workshops 107
Recommended Reading 109

Introduction

Welcome to the way of belonging—the meaningful path to unearthing your true Essence and letting your whole self experience compassionate acceptance. This workbook is an invitation to journey into the deepest parts of your identity, make peace with your inner dragons, and discover lasting peace and freedom. And when you have excavated the hidden truths and gifts within, you'll experience—perhaps for the first time—what it means to truly belong. As this new and compassionate journey of living unfolds within you, it will open a way to receiving your inherent belovedness and radiating radical compassion to a wounded world.

As a companion to *The Enneagram of Belonging* by Christopher L. Heuertz, each session of this workbook pairs with a corresponding chapter(s). This study was designed to be used either individually or in a group. In each session, you'll find:

- A summary of key concepts from the corresponding chapter(s) of *The Enneagram of Belonging*
- Graphs and charts illustrating the dynamic movements within the Enneagram
- Insightful and inspiring quotes
- Questions to lead you into self-discovery and transformational growth
- A closing reflection and discussion question

Drawing from decades of in-depth study, mentorships with Mother Teresa and Father Richard Rohr, and years of teaching the Enneagram through contemplative practice, Chris Heuertz offers a life-changing journey of making peace with your inner dragons and treasuring the innate value of your own soul.

For anyone looking to take their understanding of the Enneagram to the next level, who wants to continue the sometimes difficult but always meaningful path of wholistic transformation, this is the guide you're looking for.

INVITATIONS

Chapter three offers two contemplative invitations, which will walk you through mindful practices designed for personal and spiritual wholeness. These invitations are simple exercises designed to connect you with the presence of divine love, and may serve as helpful references as you incorporate mindfulness and meditation into your daily life. To ensure that you have an uninterrupted and meaningful contemplative experience, it is recommended that you read through the steps first before starting the exercise.

FOR PERSONAL USE

As you set out on the path of self-discovery and self-acceptance through this workbook, you will find it helpful to read the corresponding chapter(s) of *The Enneagram of Belonging* first before reflecting on the questions in each session. Alternatively, page numbers are listed throughout these pages so that you can also read *The Enneagram of Belonging* side-by-side with this workbook.

FOR GROUP USE

It is recommended that the group reads the corresponding chapters of *The Enneagram of Belonging* first before meeting to discuss the session together.

Members of the group may want to scan the chapter(s) and mark any questions that they would like to discuss together before meeting—in addition to the group discussion question at the end of each session.

Some questions will prompt readers to examine sensitive or emotionally charged memories, so it is important that the group cultivates a space where every participant feels safe—encouraged to open their hearts to others but not pressured to share anything they are not ready to share.

BEFORE YOU BEGIN

This workbook is an advanced, in-depth look at how the intricate fractals of the Enneagram unfold to teach us profound truths of who we are and why we act the way we do. If you are unsure of the basics of the Enneagram or have not yet discovered your type, it is recommended to start your journey with the precursor book *The Sacred Enneagram* by Christopher L. Heuertz.

Though there are quite a few helpful handles for each Enneagram type, this workbook refers to the types by their numbers in an effort to avoid labeling individuals by their social function rather than by the real gift of their true selves.

It is important to note that though it is tempting to categorize the people in your life through the lens of the Enneagram, typing and attempting to figure out the personality dynamics of others when they're unsure of their number or before they're ready to fully engage with the Enneagram is not a good idea. Whether accurate or not, this can be harmful to them and to your relationship. The Enneagram works best when used with grace and gentleness, primarily as a transformational tool for embracing the whole of one's Essence and coming home to true belonging.

— 1 —

The Enneagram of Belonging: Chapter 1

The Path to Belonging

There are parts of each of our identities that we feel don't belong—parts that we don't like, don't know what to do with, and don't want to make room for within ourselves. These may be memories or experiences of failures, regrets, disappointments, unmet desires, fear, doubt, and shame.

Understandably, we hide these seemingly less-than-ideal fragments of ourselves in the shadow of our subconscious, the unobserved level of our identity. But sadly, burying our fragments only allows them to grow up unobserved, into hidden dragons. These dragons guard the treasure of our true Essence—our most authentic and truest selves. [pages 22–24]

But the tragic punchline here is that if *any part* doesn't belong, then *no part* fully belongs. To discover wholistic self-acceptance, we must first learn to confront our shadow and accept the dragons within. [page 14]

Thankfully, we have the Enneagram of Personality to bring our shadowy dragons to light. And when we face our dragons, it turns out they point the way to reconnecting with our true Essence and the beautiful aspects of ourselves that many of us have forgotten. Once we can embrace the wholeness of who we are, a portal of compassionate belonging opens up—for our self and for others. [page 29]

"Courage is always the first step in the journey of belonging." [page 22]

- What thoughts and feelings surface in you when you think of letting your whole self belong?

  _____

  _____

  _____

  _____

  _____

  _____

  _____

- What aspects and traits of yourself do you instinctually try not to think about?

  _____

  _____

  _____

  _____

  _____

  _____

  _____

- Consider your first encounter with your type, and your reaction to the description of its less-flattering qualities. What was your experience when hearing these qualities about yourself?

  _____

  _____

  _____

  _____

  _____

  _____

  _____

- How do you think this habit of suppressing parts of ourselves influences your spiritual life?

_____

_____

_____

_____

_____

_____

_____

BELONG → BEHAVE → BELIEVE → BECOME

With the struggle so many of us have in extending belonging to our entire selves, could it be that we've failed to grasp what it means to fully belong, to ourselves, to each other, and ultimately, to divine love?

Beyond type, beyond personality, at our very core, we are our Essence—our soul's created purpose for being. And so, at our very core, we have always belonged. This inherent, unshakeable belonging is then always the first movement before behavior, belief, and becoming—just as children belong to their parents long before behavior and belief have formed. But many religious and social environments have unfortunately confused the order. The reverse flow—belief → behavior → belonging—can never offer true belonging, only conditional belonging. [page 27–29]

- In what way have you levied the reverse flow—belief → behavior → belonging—inward on yourself?

_____

_____

_____

_____

_____

_____

_____

- How would you order the flow of belonging as you experience it vocationally, spiritually, and relationally?

  _____

  _____

  _____

  _____

  _____

  _____

- What small steps might you begin taking to remind yourself of your place of belonging?

  _____

  _____

  _____

  _____

  _____

  _____

- In what external relationship do you feel the least amount of belonging?

  _____

  _____

  _____

  _____

  _____

  _____

- How might reconnecting to true belonging within yourself enable you to approach that relationship differently?

  _____

  _____

  _____

  _____

  _____

AN OVERVIEW OF THE ENNEAGRAM

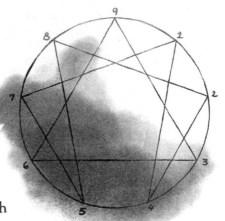

Often misunderstood as an ancient personality system or personality test, the Enneagram is a process teaching, a tool for understanding complex information. It has been used and taught for centuries in cultures, religions, wisdom schools—and only just recently in the study of personality. The Enneagram was never meant to peg us into fixed personalities with prescribed quirks and tendencies, but to *invite* us into rich and meaningful growth through self-awareness. [page 29, 45]

The Enneagram offers nine roadmaps for how we get lost and disconnected from our souls' created purpose. It also shows us how we *stay* lost, each type's specific set of addictive patterns that keep us from embracing all that we truly are. This cycle of patterns forms our personality structure. In this way, the Enneagram gives us a start to understanding who we are, yet it goes much further than mere fixed personality by showing us the dynamic way we can grow toward true belonging. [page 31]

"What the general population wants is an accessible Enneagram that describes quirks and caricatures of individuality. But what we *need* is a map that points us back to an integrated experience of radical self-acceptance." [page 45]

- In what ways have you felt boxed in by the misunderstanding of your Enneagram type as a fixed set of personality traits?

_____

_____

_____

_____

_____

_____

_____

- In what ways has the Enneagram already helped you begin the journey of belonging?

_____

_____

_____

_____

_____

_____

_____

_____

_____

_____

_____

INTELLIGENCE CENTERS AND BELONGING

The Intelligence Centers form the backdrop for all types. They explain the three ways types perceive and process reality: through the body, heart, and head. Though every person has and utilizes all three centers, every type is dominant in just one. Understanding which Intelligence Center we lean on awakens us to our innate bias and introduces us to other ways of relating to the world. [pages 32, 37]

The Enneagram types are organized with the Intelligence Center in groupings of three. [page 33]

- The Instinctive Center for Body Types: Eight, Nine, and One
- The Emotional Center for Heart Types: Two, Three, and Four
- The Intellectual Center for Head Types: Five, Six, and Seven

George Ivanovitch Gurdjieff, a forefather of the Enneagram of Personality, suggested that only by simultaneously integrating all three centers could we access true spiritual experiences. With intention and compassion we can find our way to three-centered awareness which balances embodied experience, heartfulness, and mindfulness. [page 32]

The Instinctive Center (Eight, Nine, One)

This Center gives Body Types effortless access to their innate intuitive awareness. They naturally pick up on the instinctive responses and energy expressed by others. Sometimes difficult to articulate, this center is an actual intelligence felt in the body, often expressed as a knowing in the gut. At times physically draining, this awareness can be a visceral response to the too-muchness of life which triggers Body Type's most accessible emotions of frustration and anger. [page 33–34]

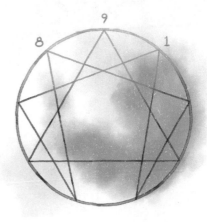

BODY~GUT~INSTINCTIVE

The Emotional Center (Two, Three, Four)

The emotional center gives Heart Types genuine sensitivity to the emotional well-being of those around them, often seeming to be able to feel what everyone but themselves feels. Though often warm and sympathetic presences, Heart Types can be overwhelmed by swimming in an emotional sea. This sense of being overwhelmed, coupled with their drive to make deep connections, can trigger their most accessible emotions of guilt and shame. [page 34]

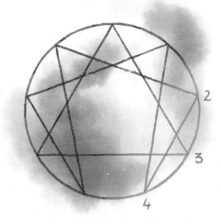

HEART~FEELING~EMOTION

The Intellectual Center (Five, Six, Seven)

This center gives Head Types their clever cerebral adeptness of analysis, conjecture, speculation, forecasting, and planning. Head Types constantly sort and assimilate every aspect of the data they collect—information, safety measures, or experiences. But living within the cerebral world often leads to overthinking, mental paralysis, obsessive worrying, or preoccupation. These imbalances trigger Head Type's most accessible emotions of anxiety and distress. [page 35]

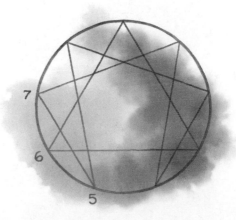

HEAD~INTELLECTUAL~THINKING

Each type relates to its Intelligence Center in a different way—creating a repeating pattern around the Enneagram circle.

The first number of each center (Eight, Two, and Five) amplifies their center.

The second number of each center (Nine, Three, and Six) suppresses their center.

The third number of each center (One, Four, and Seven) idealizes their center.

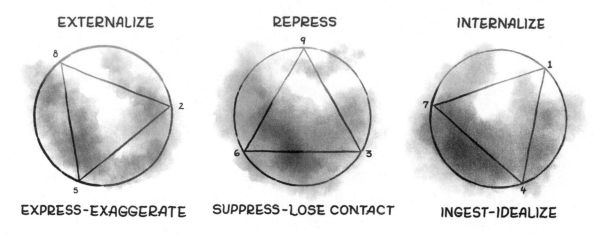

EXTERNALIZE	REPRESS	INTERNALIZE
EXPRESS-EXAGGERATE	SUPPRESS-LOSE CONTACT	INGEST-IDEALIZE

> "We don't see things as they are, we see them as we are."
> —Anaïs Nin [page 37]

These three centers are always at play within each of us but not always integrated. And when we overuse any one of our Intelligence Centers, something vital is lost. But becoming aware of our most neglected center opens up the path to experiencing the fullness and depth of ourselves, of every moment, and every relationship. [page 37]

Ordering of Centers

The Enneagram forms three isosceles triangles oriented from the types that suppress their Intelligence Centers. These triangles, which reveal the neglected centers of the types, include:

Nine, Four, and Five repress the Instinctive Center.

Three, Seven, and Eight repress the Emotional Center.

Six, One, and Two repress the Intellectual Center. [page 38]

REPRESSED INTELLIGENCE CENTERS

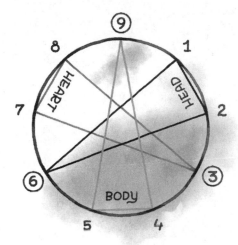

Identifying your dominant center and repressed center reveals your secondary center. For example, type One is a Body type and dominant in the Instinctive Center. It represses the Intellectual Center (along with types Six and Two). And its secondary center is the Emotional Center. Our secondary center simultaneously works to sustain our dominant center and holds back our repressed center. [page 40]

- Your dominant center: _____

- Your secondary center: _____

- Your repressed center: _____

> "The intelligence of these three Centers offer us the ability
> to grasp what we've already had, what we already know, and
> what we've always been able to access." [page 43]

The interplay of these centers within each type shapes the way we see the world and forms the foundation for each person's Enneagram type. More than temperament, understanding that type as the intelligent design for how these three centers relate within us reminds us that personality is a meaningful, mysterious, and spiritual thing. [page 41]

Awakening to the unique ordering of our Intelligence Centers allows us to steward what we already know and access the resources we've had all along. [page 42]

Type One	Emotionally reinforces their intuition while containing reasoning.
Type Two	Instinctively supports their emotional awareness while stifling rational faculties.
Type Three	Fuses their intuitive awareness with impartial objectivity while suspending their feelings.
Type Four	Objectively braces their affecting emotions while quelling their body intelligence.
Type Five	Acknowledges their sensitivities to confirm their analytical reasoning while cautioning their instincts.
Type Six	Vacillates between intuitive instincts and their heightened sensitiveness while maintaining suspicion toward their reasoning.
Type Seven	Intuitively confirms their logic while rejecting access to their emotions.
Type Eight	Rationally justifies their intuition while denying access to their feelings.
Type Nine	Merges their emotional sensitives with a grounded objectivity while abnegating their gut reactions.

- What strengths and benefits does your dominant Intelligence Center give you?

_____

_____

_____

_____

_____

_____

- In what way has your repressed center been stifled, ignored, or discounted in your internal world?

  _____

  _____

  _____

  _____

  _____

  _____

- How have you experienced your secondary center at play in your life?

  _____

  _____

  _____

  _____

  _____

  _____

- Remembering that with the Enneagram we can only take others as far as we go ourselves [page 55], spend a few minutes determining your approach and posture with others when talking about the Enneagram.

  _____

  _____

  _____

  _____

  _____

  _____

  _____

> "True belonging doesn't require you to change who
> you are; it requires you to be who you are."
> —*Brené Brown*, Braving the Wilderness
> *(Random House, New York, 2017, page 56)*

REFLECTION OR DISCUSSION QUESTION

- As a group or on your own, reflect on the social environments you spend the most time in—work, faith community, family, and friend groups. In what order is the flow of belonging reinforced? Perhaps through forgiveness, an apology, a kind word, or simple gesture, what opportunities are there for you to extend belonging in your social circles?

_____

_____

_____

_____

_____

_____

_____

_____

_____

— 2 —

The Enneagram of Belonging: Chapters 2–5

Beyond Type

Since learning the inner workings of your personality type can be such a rewarding journey of self-discovery and inner liberation, it's imperative to establish an honest relationship with your Enneagram type.

We tend to either love and boast about our type or feel a great bit of unease with the more unfavorable aspects of what type confirms about us.

Carrying a sense of pride about your type doesn't always mean you have a healthy relationship with it. On the contrary, what enamors you about your type could simply keep you fixated on its addictive patterns. [page 60] A healthy relationship with your type cultivates a nuanced honesty about both the good and the bad, while recognizing the good news that you are so much more than your type. At your truest, purest self, you are your Essence—the true identity you were born to be, apart from the limitations and shaping of your presenting personality.

> "Loving yourself requires you hold all aspects of yourself with honest compassion, making room for the positive as well as the negative aspects to belong." [page 60]

- How would you describe the health of your relationship with your type? [page 60]

_____

_____

_____

_____

- What aspects of your type are you proud of?

_____

_____

_____

_____

- What aspects of your type are you embarrassed, ashamed, or afraid of? What aspects do you find difficult to allow to belong with the whole? [page 60]

_____

_____

_____

_____

- The parts that enamor us about our type could simply keep us stuck in addictive patterns. How have you seen this play out in your life? [page 60]

_____

_____

_____

_____

- How might you practice more honesty and belonging in the way you relate to your type?

_____

_____

_____

_____

> "You're not your type. You *have* a type, but you're not your type."
> —*Russ Hudson [page 60]*

The Passion of our Enneagram type is the way our type suffers the unbearable ache of having lost contact with our Essence. The invitation is to move from understanding how we suffer to practicing conscious sympathy for our own inner agony. Practicing self-compassion in this way allows for the heartache to exist without having to fix it or letting it define us. [page 63]

- How do you receive this good news that you are more than your type, and that the truest you is found in your Essence?

_____

_____

_____

_____

_____

- What is your initial reaction to your type's Passion?

_____

_____

_____

_____

- What feelings and thoughts arise in you when you consider embracing the way your type suffers the loss of your Essence?

_____

_____

_____

_____

_____

The coping patterns and addictions of our type open our eyes to the prison in which we live, but living *beyond type* is embracing our true freedom. Resisting the temptation to penalize our suffering wakes us up to the message that it's always been sending: embracing our sufferings allows for our souls to reconnect with our Essence. [page 65]

- Because we don't know what to do with our suffering, we have to hide it, or lock it up, but what ends up imprisoned is the freest part of who we've always been. [page 64] Consider how this has been true for you.

  _____

  _____

  _____

  _____

  _____

- In what ways have you penalized your pain or suffering?

  _____

  _____

  _____

  _____

  _____

> "Describing the thickness of my prison walls doesn't
> help take them down." [page 64]

KIDLIFE CRISIS

Also known as the childhood wound, the Kidlife Crisis occurred when at a very early age we experienced a loss of innocence and a disconnect from our true Essence, our soul's divine purpose for existing. It was an accident of not being loved perfectly while simultaneously not being able to receive love perfectly. [page 71]

These Kidlife Crises that we all experience are the purest cries of our hearts to be filled with love. It's important to note that these Crises may indeed be just that—a true crisis with very real wounds and trauma experienced in our imperfect early holding environments. [page 69]

But it can also be a tragic misunderstanding as a child *perceives* they are not loved in the way they most need to be loved. The Kidlife Crisis is a compassionate reframing of the traditional Childhood Wounds, recognizing that even in the most loving relationships we couldn't possibly receive all the love we're given. Our Kidlife Crisis is the confirmation bias that we are imperfect and imperfectly loved. [page 69]

To cope with this pain, we learn to wear masks—sophisticated and conditioned patterns which accumulate into personality. [page 62] It's important to note that the pain of our early years is not the source of our type. We bring our type to contend with our imperfect experiences. [page 70]

Our Kidlife Crisis was not a *real* wound inflicted on us intentionally or unintentionally; it was pain-filled misunderstandings. The pain is real, but the wounds are confused memories.

When we extend belonging to our Kidlife Crisis, we can understand our own inevitable suffering as an essential stage in *becoming.* [page 69]

- How does reframing your Kidlife Crisis as an inevitable accident of loving and being loved imperfectly shift the way you view yourself? How does it shift the way you view those close to you?

  _____

  _____

  _____

  _____

- As you've come to understand your particular Kidlife Crisis, what invitation does it offer you in reconciling with your parent or caregiver? [page 69]

  _____

  _____

  _____

  _____

Each of us was born with a gift that will heal the world when we're in sync with our destined reason for being. But our Kidlife Crisis jarred us out of this purpose and type inevitably showed up in one of nine different, precisely patterned ways.

- What emotions and thoughts arise in you when you consider that you were born with a purposed destiny for being alive and here?

  _____

  _____

  _____

  _____

  _____

- What messages or conditions about love did you internalize from your caregivers?

  _____

  _____

  _____

  _____

  _____

- When was the last time you felt connected with your Essence, your purposed reason for existing? What were you doing; what were you experiencing?

  _____

  _____

  _____

  _____

  _____

- On page 71, we learn about the multiple points in our lives when we might experience an identity crisis. Briefly reflect on each of the times you've had this experience.

  _____

  _____

  _____

  _____

- With each of your identity crises, how did you draw away from or reconnect with your Essence?

_____

_____

_____

_____

_____

_____

_____

THE NINE TYPES AND KIDLIFE CRISES

THE INNER CONFLICT OF EACH TYPE'S KIDLIFE CRISIS [PAGE 71]

Type One	Compliance Check	Flexible Standards vs. Inflexible Fears
Type Two	Care Collision	Nurturing vs. Protective Love
Type Three	Closeness (Con)Fusion	Veneration vs. Adoration (Respect vs. Love)
Type Four	Credibility Complex	Authenticity vs. Accuracy
Type Five	Controlled Constraint	Inside vs. Outside Containment
Type Six	Concern Collusion	Inner vs. Outer Authority Angst
Type Seven	Crush Collection	Empty Heart vs. Full Imagination
Type Eight	Conflicted Conversion	Arrested vs. Accelerated Childhood
Type Nine	Compassion Compromise	Expressed vs. Repressed Love

The combination of our dominant, secondary, and suppressed Intelligence Centers clues us in to our Enneagram type's Basic Fear, sparked by our Kidlife Crisis. This unique combination sets the stage for our idiosyncrasies.

As you read through the types and the misunderstandings of giving and receiving imperfect love, remember to hold compassion for yourself and other players within your story. It is also important to remember that as unique individuals, made of the same atoms as the stars in our galaxies, the holders of untold potential, and born with profound belonging to Love itself, we are more than mere type. [page 85–86]

Type One with Compliance Check

Holy Idea	Holy Perfection
Virtue	Serenity
Basic Desire	To be good, to have integrity
Basic Fear	Being bad, imbalanced, defective, corrupt
Fixation	Resentment
Passion	Anger

Honorable, responsible, honest, consistent, hard-working, reliable, and full of integrity, Ones strive for principled excellence as moral duty. This comes from their Basic Fear of somehow being irredeemable or morally corrupt.

Incredibly disciplined, you can always count Ones to follow through on commitments. The downside to this shows up when we fail in the promises *we've* made to Ones. Among the initiating types of the Enneagram, Ones are extremely decisive. Because they are in the Instinctive Center, their clear decisiveness is usually on point. Their inner critic may be the most severe of all Enneagram types and so they already know what they've messed up or failed at, which means criticism sears their soul. So be gentle and forgiving when you need to point something out to them. [page 86]

Type One's Compliance Check: Flexible Standards vs. Inflexible Fears

Born to be a source of goodness to the world, Ones have a profound fear of being irredeemably corrupt. Early on, they intuited that they would need to earn love through compliance to their caregivers' expectations. But the flexibility of their home environment and the unpredictable expectations of their caregivers clashed against their inflexible fear. Ones devised inner standards of perfection as a safeguard against corruption and a hope to be worthy of love. [page 72]

Type Two with Compliance Check

Holy Idea	Holy Will, Holy Freedom
Virtue	Humility
Basic Desire	To feel love
Basic Fear	Being unloved
Fixation	Flattery
Passion	Pride

Nurturing, devoted, empathetic, generous, supportive, other-focused, and helpful, Twos strive for lavish love through self-sacrifice. Those dominant in type Two spend a considerable amount of their energy caring for others better than they do themselves.

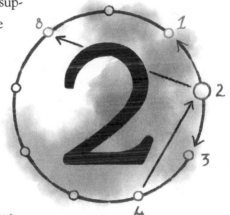

In a sense, it seems like everything in their being is inviting others into a warm embrace where Essence can be seen, known, held, and affirmed. Those in relationships with Twos must remember to not simply take without finding caring ways to give back to them.

Because Twos have explored the inner landscape of their own hearts, they carry the potential to be a midwife to our emotional truth. So listen carefully when they offer to help navigate the complexities of your feelings. [page 87]

The Kidlife Crisis for Twos took the shape of a care collision between the nurturing and protective forms of love. Naturally gifted with generous nurturing love, they gave everyone in their emotional orbit permission to share their hearts. But at one point, a caregiver expressed protective love in hopes of shielding the Twos' openheartedness. Twos misunderstood this protection as rejection and doubled down in nurturing love to win over the heart of their caregiver. [page 73]

Type Two's Care Collision: Nurturing vs. Protective Love

Type Three with Compliance Check

Holy Idea	Holy Harmony, Holy Law, Holy Hope
Virtue	Truthfulness, Authenticity
Basic Desire	To feel valuable
Basic Fear	Being worthless
Fixation	Vanity
Passion	Deceit

Determined, ambitious, calculated, driven, competitive, practical, confident, and efficient, Threes strive for appreciative recognition through curated successes.

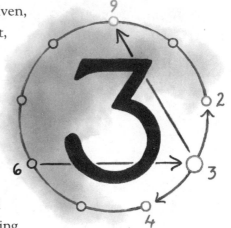

Threes have a remarkable ability to adapt to their climate, culture, or community expectations with instant effortless smoothness. This exposes their deep need for connections made through recognition, affirmation, or affiliation. Self-controlled and reserved, they imagine they're not allowed to bring all their self forward because it might be too much for others. For Threes to come home to the gift of their truest selves, they must learn there is absolutely nothing they have to do based on anyone else's expectations.

Type Three's Closeness (Con) Fusion: Veneration vs. Adoration

In relationships with Threes, give room for them to shine while also giving them space to fail. Don't forget they need affirmation, especially for the behind the scenes contributions they make. [page 88]

As little kids, Threes quickly learned that good performances are positively rewarded. Affirmation became the low-hanging fruit substitute for real love which led to a confusion between admiration and genuine connection. Fusing the emptiness of their hearts with the closest nurturing heart they can find, they give themselves over to a never-ending journey of accomplishments to secure the love they desire. [page 74]

Type Four with Compliance Check

Holy Idea	Holy Origin
Virtue	Equanimity, Emotional Balance
Basic Desire	To be themselves
Basic Fear	Having no identity or significance
Fixation	Melancholy
Passion	Envy

Sensitive, expressive, compassionate, introspective, sympathetic, idealistic, pensive, and emotionally attuned, Fours strive for the discovery of identity through faithful authenticity.

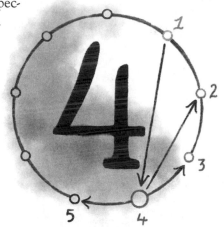

Deep within, there is a desire to see what is beautiful and fabulous in the world as an attempt to mirror back to themselves what might be beautiful within. Generally mistaken as introverted, Fours tend to turn inward in hopes of discovering the unique source of their being.

Subconsciously many Fours feel as if they've been abandoned, so they withdraw in relationships as a way to prove that narrative to themselves. In relationships with Fours, honor their boundaries, but prove your commitments through acceptance and patience, and validate honestly what is exceptional in them. [page 90]

Fours have the gift of attuning to every beautiful detail in everything they encounter—everything and everyone but themselves. Unable to recognize their own beauty stirs a deep sense of frustration which is aimed at both the nurturing and protective

Type Four's Complexity Confusion: Authenticity vs. Accuracy

caregivers. Fours perceive love to be withheld, and frame this as the reason they are unable to discover the beauty of their own authentic selves, which is the love they desire and the love they were born to share. [page 75]

Type Five with Compliance Check

Holy Idea	Holy Omniscience, Holy Transparency
Virtue	Detachment
Basic Desire	To be capable and competent
Basic Fear	Being helpless, incompetent, and incapable
Fixation	Stinginess
Passion	Avarice

Objective, insightful, steady, thoughtful, systematic, detached, eccentric, and fiercely independent, Fives strive for decisive clarity through thoughtful conclusions.

With determined concentration, Fives can give themselves over to thorough evaluation and analysis of any subject. But this can lead to fascination that borders on obsession. Fives have limited energy so they need to know in advance what is expected of them in order to budget their energy accordingly. Fives are extremely private people with the most boundaries of any type. When a Five opens up to you, be patient for their thorough processing—whether it be internal or external. Once you earn the trust of a Five, you may never know a more generous and faithful companion.

Make sure to find creative and thoughtful ways to love the Fives in your life. [page 91]

Type Five's Controlled Constraint: Inside vs. Outside Containment

Generally, little Fives were fairly self-contained and possessed an uncanny sense of self-control. Relieved caregivers presumed the Fives required less shielding oversight and care than perhaps another sibling. But the parental support of their independence caused Fives to wonder what was wrong with them that they were treated differently. To attempt to understand this dynamic, Fives inwardly analyzed their concerns and concluded they were actually fine and that the problem lay with their caregivers. This pattern set off a revolving door of unintended rejection. [page 76]

Type Six with Compliance Check

Holy Idea	Holy Strength, Holy Faith
Virtue	Courage
Basic Desire	To have support and guidance
Basic Fear	Being without support and guidance
Fixation	Cowardice
Passion	Fear

Faithful, collaborative, dependable, reassuring, loyal, conscientious, trustworthy, and community-minded, Sixes strive for steady constancy through confident loyalty.

Steadfast and committed, once a Six makes a promise, it's unthinkable to them to break it. They imagine that if they prove their allegiances, then perhaps they can earn reciprocal devotion. Sixes are always thinking through worst-case scenarios as a way of searching out potential dangers—an incredibly taxing preoccupation which can drum up a lot of anxiety. This is fueled by a subconscious desire to ensure stability and safety for loved ones.

Once aligned with the truth of their own inner strength, Sixes are wise and courageous, and we'll follow them wherever they lead us. But remember to listen to the subtext of their warnings because Sixes are usually right when they express concern. [page 93]

Type Six's Concern
Collusion: Inner vs. Outer Authority Angst

Sixes prioritize stability and security and naturally, threat-forecasting and worst-case scenario planning are the ways they love those they care about. Young sixes longed for their protective caregiver to allay their suspicions of potential dangers, but no one can dispel their fears for them. Disappointed and feeling let down, Sixes turned inward to an anxious inner-authority in an attempt to overcome their concerns. They sadly deny themselves inner stability and security by internalizing their outlandish potential fears as a way to protectively love those around them. [page 77]

Type Seven with Compliance Check

Holy Idea	Holy Wisdom, Holy Work, Holy Plan
Virtue	Sobriety
Basic Desire	To be satisfied
Basic Fear	Being trapped in pain and deprivation
Fixation	Planning
Passion	Gluttony

Curious, energetic, charming, playful, imaginative, optimistic, spontaneous, upbeat, adventurous, and fast-thinking problem solvers, Sevens strive for imaginative freedom through inspired independence.

Likable and relatable, they naturally find connections with others partly to bring us along on their adventures, but also because they're looking outside to find what seems to be missing inside.

Because they have such quick minds they can be misunderstood as bored, too playful, or sarcastic. So remember to take Sevens seriously and encourage them to connect with their own hearts—the source of their abundant potential and the place they most avoid.

Sevens are on the run from the pain in their hearts, and it's difficult for them to be present. But they will find what they long for when they're honest about what they're missing. [page 94]

Type Seven's Crush Collection: Empty Heart vs. Full Imagination

Despite the difficulty they experience in connecting with their hearts, Sevens deeply want to be loved. Early on, Sevens projected this idealization for love outside themselves and reached for the heart of a nurturing caregiver to help them connect with their own heart. High-energy and fast thinkers, Sevens consume as many distractions and novelties as their imaginations enable them to so that they can avoid entering their own hearts and face the pain within which they fear may be too much to bear. Their Kidlife Crisis is one of running away from inner agony, while externally they run away from commitments that could potentially bring forth the healing they need. [page 78]

Type Eight with Compliance Check

Holy Idea	Holy Truth
Virtue	Innocence
Basic Desire	To protect themselves
Basic Fear	Being harmed, controlled, and violated
Fixation	Vengeance
Passion	Lust

Powerful, active, impulsive, direct, assertive, strong, truthful, protective, and justice-oriented, Eights strive for impassioned intensity for unfettered autonomy.

Eights are magnanimous, larger than life kinds of people. The love they offer others is intense as they project the concern and care into their environments that they need and long to extend to their own inner vulnerabilities.

Impulsive and determined, Eights will force their way, opinion, or energy on those whom they perceive lack confidence. They test others, pushing to see who will stand up and fight back. Those who don't back down earn their respect and protection.

Eights are as tenacious as they seem but not as tough as they present. They are looking for safety and permission to explore their own inner tenderness. So make sure you extend great care when an Eight opens up. [page 96]

Type Eight's Conflict Conversion: Arrested vs. Accelerated Childhood

Young Eights grew up too quickly or had to present an older and stronger version of who they actually were. But rather than maturing, that experience fossilized a young, tender part of them that never fully developed. As grownups, the residue of this Kidlife Crisis shows up in their inability to control their innocence causing them to act out of that tender pain and heartbreak by presenting as combative or lewd, degenerate or contrarian. [page 79]

Type Nine with Compliance Check

Holy Idea	Holy Love
Virtue	Action
Basic Desire	Peace of mind and wholeness
Basic Fear	Loss, separation, and fragmentation
Fixation	Indolence
Passion	Sloth

Conciliatory, peace-filled, stable, easy-going, understanding, self-effacing, balanced, affable, receptive, accepting, and patient, Nines strive for inner harmony and peace.

Nines are determined not to be disruptive in their environments. But when they oblige, they subconsciously stuff down something they deeply care about.

They make room for everyone and every opinion as an external expression of their deep-seated fear that their interior life is fragmented. If they bring harmony to their external world, Nines believe it will bring order to their internal world. Pushing them beyond what they have energy for is perceived as a violation so be warned that they work on a different timeline and for different motivations.

In relationships, give Nines space and autonomy. Otherwise, the Nine can no longer own the gift of their self that they offer others and everyone loses. [page 97]

Type Nine's Compassion Compromise: Expressed vs. Repressed Love

Nines were born to be a source of love. Their intuitive attunement to love focused outward as loving inwardly seemed selfish. Nines prioritized the needs of those around them at the expense of their own wants and desires. But loving everyone else only lead to repressing love for themselves, something they never forgot. The denial of their own needs is the very source of their hidden resentment and dormant anger. [page 80]

Acknowledging and accepting our Kidlife Crisis is key to accepting the whole of our unique stories.

- Briefly rewrite the description of your Kidlife Crisis with the details of your own experience.

_____

_____

_____

_____

_____

- What thoughts and feelings does this reflection on your Kidlife Crisis bring up for you?

_____

_____

_____

_____

- How does your Kidlife Crisis echo the pure gifts and innocent desires you bring to the world?

_____

_____

_____

_____

_____

- How do the coping mechanisms born through your Kidlife Crisis continue to shape your decisions today?

_____

_____

_____

_____

"My resistance to my own vulnerability made it impossible for me to make peace with what still hurt my inner child's heart." [page 83]

• In what way do you resist your own vulnerability?

_____

_____

_____

_____

_____

• How does the story of Bimala [page 83] inspire you to extend compassion for your inner child?

_____

_____

_____

_____

_____

• As you look over the descriptions of the other types, what gifts do you want to learn and emulate?

_____

_____

_____

_____

_____

• What do you wish others understood about your type?

_____

_____

_____

_____

_____

• What is the most challenging aspect of your type to extend belonging to?

_____

_____

_____

_____

TYPE WITH WINGS

Something that sets the Enneagram apart from other character structure systems is the dynamic quality it has. There are lots of moving parts at play in and around the circle, the first of which are Wings. [page 100]

Type + Wing	Enneagram Institute Name
One wing Nine	The Idealist
One wing Two	The Advocate
Two wing One	The Servant
Two wing Three	The Host or Hostess
Three wing Two	The Charmer or Star
Three wing Four	The Professional
Four wing Three	The Aristocrat
Four wing Five	The Bohemian
Five wing Four	The Iconoclast
Five wing Six	The Problem-Solver
Six wing Five	The Defender
Six wing Seven	The Buddy
Seven wing Six	The Entertainer
Seven wing Eight	The Realist
Eight wing Seven	The Independent or Maverick
Eight wing Nine	The Bear
Nine wing Eight	The Referee
Nine wing One	The Philosopher or Dreamer

[page 103]

- At what times do you tend to lean into your clockwise wing?

_____

_____

_____

_____

_____

_____

- At what times do you tend to lean into your counterclockwise wing?

_____

_____

_____

_____

_____

_____

- How has the dynamic and balance between your wings shifted throughout your lifetime?

_____

_____

_____

_____

_____

_____

- What aspect of your wing relationships needs an extension of your self-acceptance?

_____

_____

_____

_____

_____

_____

WINGS AND PASSIONS

While there are many wing theories, type may actually be the *aggregation* of its clockwise wing falling into its counterclockwise wing—a leapfrog game of sorts. This is most clearly depicted in the Enneagram's Passion.

- For example, what is *lust* for type Eight if it's not mere lazy (Nine) gluttony (Seven), a substitution of thoughtless desire for true love?

- And *gluttony* for Seven is simply lust (Eight) falling into fear (Six), the voracious concern that there won't be enough so the intense drive to consume it all.

- A Six *fear* then becomes gluttonous (Seven) greed (Five), a selfish loss of courage fortified by insatiable concern for more than one already has.

- For Fives *avarice* is concocted when fear (Six) falls into envy (Four), an anxious jealousy that greedily grabs for more.

- Four's *envy* is nothing short of greed (Five) tumbling into vanity (Naranjo swapped type Three's Passion and fixation), illustrating that conceited, acquisitive selfishness produces jealousy, as if one deserves what they want.

- The *vanity* of Three is clearly the product of envious (Four) pride (Two); it's an inflated view of self, derived from jealous arrogance.

- Two's *pride* then is conflated when vanity (Three) falls into anger (One), a kind of contemptuousness that only conceited resentment allows for.

- One's *anger* can be understood in the mixing of prideful (Two) laziness (Nine) or viewing resentment as indolent arrogance.

- Finally, the Nine's *sloth* is formed when anger (One) falls into lust (Eight) because annoyed intensity is just lazy Passion. [page 104]

- Reflect on the aggregation of your wings' Passions in the list above. What does this combined compulsion illuminate about yourself?

_____

_____

_____

_____

_____

- Our Passion is the unique way our hearts suffer the pain of our stifled Virtue. Reflect on how you might extend self-compassion toward your type's Passion?

_____

_____

_____

_____

_____

- Which of the debunked misconceptions about Integration and Disintegration created the biggest shift in your understanding? [page 106–109]

_____

_____

_____

_____

_____

INNER FLOW

As we look closer at the dynamic lines within the Enneagram, perhaps our type is not so much a fixed point on the circle, but an identity that glides on the spectrum somewhere along the way. With this theory, we understand how we come to possess energies or aspects of *all* the nine types. [page 113]

Like an echo in a canyon, the Inner Flow lines within the Enneagram are the echo of our souls moving from one point to the next. Eventually, these echoes find their way to our dominant type, allowing us to incorporate qualities of each of them into our identities. [page 115]

- How have you seen aspects or energies of the other types along your type's inner flow lines show up in your life?

  _____

  _____

  _____

  _____

  _____

  _____

- What gifts from other types have you flavored your type with?

  _____

  _____

  _____

  _____

  _____

  _____

- Far from being fixed personalities, the Enneagram charts a dynamic path to growth and wholeness. How does this encourage you in the path to self-belonging?

  _____

  _____

  _____

  _____

  _____

  _____

"The work of becoming is not closing the gap but connecting the circle of life by bringing together two aspects of our selves that seem diametrically opposed." [page 122]

UNIQUE LUMINARY ROLES

The Enneagram highlights how every type plays a unique role in showing the other types how the journey of transformation, becoming all that we can be, is first a movement of belonging.

And as we learn to make room for the whole of ourselves, we can then manifest more wholeness, and ultimately, more Essence in the world. [page 118]

> "To the extent we are transformed, the world can be transformed."
> —*Phileena Heuertz [page 118]*

We see the luminary roles of each type as they step down both sides of the circle.

Three, Six, and Nine show what integration looks like when they incorporate their lost center. They teach us that the very thing we long for, which seems so far away, is often waiting for us within all along. [page 118]

One and Eight sit at the top with all the intensity Nine seems to have forgotten. Both carry initiating forces and strong energies, Eights charging outward and Ones leveling inward. When they embrace the gifts of their personality, they show us that innocent goodness is not only the most valued quality in our world, but it carries immense inner and external transformational power. [page 119]

Two and Seven are the only types that do not share a natural connection with all three Intelligence Centers—Twos do not have a direct connection to the Head Center and Sevens do not have a direct connection with the Heart Center. They teach us that inner growth always transforms seemingly dead places into new life. [page 119]

Fours and Fives guard the *Existential Hole* between the Head and the Heart Centers. When they pioneer the journey from the head to the heart, and the heart to the head, they show us that true becoming is not about being perfect but about bringing all disparate parts of ourselves into heartful and mindful belonging. [page 120]

> "Life itself is the process of becoming. So we are invited to bring everything, even the most disparate parts of ourselves, into belonging." [page 122]

• What feelings and thoughts arise in you as you read your type's unique luminary role?

_____

_____

_____

_____

• How have you already seen your luminary role at play in your work, family, and social circles?

_____

_____

_____

_____

• How can you continue embracing this bright truth for yourself and others in your life?

_____

_____

_____

_____

_____

REFLECTION OR DISCUSSION QUESTION

- Read about the two theories of the *Existential Hole* between the Head and the Heart Centers on page 120–122. How have you seen humanity's struggle to journey between the Head and the Heart in your own experience, in your immediate social circles, and the world? How can we begin to help one another bridge this gap more fluidly in our communities?

_____

_____

_____

_____

_____

_____

_____

_____

_____

_____

— 3 —

The Enneagram of Belonging:
Chapters 6–7

Belonging for the Mind

I n every great story, there is always a cave scene. The cave is a symbolic and essential stop in the pilgrimage to true belonging. The problem is, we generally won't go there willingly. It takes a crisis to lead us to the cave where we can then remember and embrace who we really are. Our journeys into these caves are full of signs pointing to the complexities of what can be lost and what can be found in the shadows of ourselves. [page 125]

In the journey of remembering our soul's created purpose, there's a cave each of us must enter. It's a cave that requires courage, yet within a buried treasure awaits—the treasure of a lost part of our true self. Our inner child is eager to accompany us into these cavernous, shadowy places so that the truth of our identity can be recovered and embraced. [page 129]

- Reflect on the caves your personal journey has led you to throughout your lifetime. Write a sentence or two about what led you to the cave, and your discovery. As you reflect, remember to extend self-compassion for your former self and past decisions.

_____

_____

_____

_____

_____

- As you've journeyed this far, what lost parts of your true self do you sense are calling out for your attention and acceptance?

_____

_____

_____

_____

_____

- What challenges might you encounter by embracing these lost pieces of yourself? What challenges would they bring into your relationships?

_____

_____

_____

_____

_____

- What gifts might you discover by embracing these lost pieces of yourself? What gifts would they bring into your relationships?

_____

_____

_____

_____

_____

HOLY IDEAS

Drawn from the teachings of Óscar Ichazo, the Holy Ideas are a key foundational component that make up our Essence. The opposite of Fixations, Holy Ideas are the mind's unobstructed, objective views of reality. [page 130]

Aligning with the truest version of ourselves and the gift we were born to bring forward into the world requires a compassionate clarity of our own mental landscape. It demands we tell ourselves the truth, and the Holy Ideas are the first truth we need to tell ourselves.

At some point in our life, we will have to decide if we will follow the innocence of our inner child into the cave of our soul, face our shadow, and be transformed by our Holy Idea—or will we stay stuck in the patterns that keep us in the dark? Though we all want to experience true belonging, few of us are willing to do the messy work necessary for the process. After all, to unearth buried treasure, our hands are bound to get dirty. [page 131]

To recover our Holy Ideas, we start with the ABCs.

- *Affirmation,* the assertion of our inner truth which our soul longs to reconnect with.

- *Belief,* the celebrated acceptance of our truth that leads to freedom.

- *Confession,* the acknowledgment of these divine thoughts as necessary for transformation. [page 132]

"Accepting our Holy Ideas is the painful yet ultimately rewarding process of excavating our lost Essence. It all begins with telling ourselves the truth." [page 131]

Type One

Traditional Holy Idea	Holy Perfection
Affirmation	I am complete. I celebrate my imperfections.
Belief	I believe there is a divinely compassionate intrinsic perfection of love within.
Confession	I accept what is, as it is, starting with my perfectly flawed self.

The concept of perfection cannot lead to precise experiences of exactness or correctness. Ones are complete just as they are; nothing more or less is required of them than to merely *be*. Ones who learn to find beauty in their flaws join the rest of humanity, making room for all of us as they've made room for all of themselves. [page 133]

"God is not as hard on you as you are on yourself." [page 133]

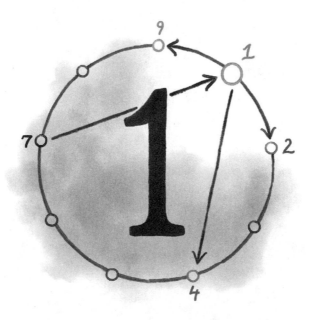

Type Two

Traditional Holy Idea	Holy Will, Holy Freedom
Affirmation	I am a co-creator with love.
Belief	I believe there is unconditional freedom to be loved and to love.
Confession	I willingly release all obligations to my sense of indispensability.

Humility is not a means to an end; it is the passageway through which a soul journeys toward its truest source of strength: its will. Twos who embrace their divine humility are able to will their fecundity in relationships, never apart from the other, allowing themselves to need without being needy. Moving from humiliation to honor is the move from self-importance to self-love. [page 134]

"As a virtue, humility is the principle that flows from love." [page 134]

Type Three

Traditional Holy Idea	Holy Hope, Holy Law, Holy Harmony
Affirmation	I am changed by love.
Belief	I believe there is an inherent value in all souls.
Confession	I embrace the permanence of my value that cannot be earned.

The mind creates compassionate order and Threes align with this when they accept the belovedness of their entire being without having to change or justify this truth. Instead, they are changed by it. They align with transformation not as a one-time accomplishment but an ever-evolving conversion process of constantly returning and remembering their unchangeable value. [page 135]

> "Here they discover they cannot change themselves to be loved, for they are inherently and unconditionally loved as they are." [page 135]

Type Four

Traditional Holy Idea	Holy Origin
Affirmation	I am connected to love.
Belief	I believe there is a divine source in all life.
Confession	I am conscious of compassionate belonging.

If we affirm all people are significant because of their holy origin, then we likewise affirm no one is without a basis for belonging and meaning. The emotional ache to locate source in the soul of Fours is the evidence that source exists. Connecting with the source of love requires connecting with self, accepting oneself, and allowing oneself to be loved unconditionally. [page 136]

"Connection is the echo of love reverberating from one soul to the next—being without doing." [page 136]

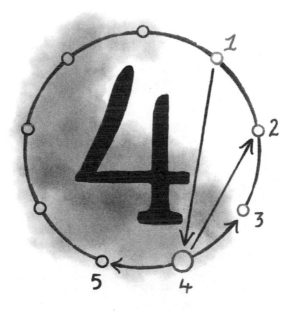

Type Five

Traditional Holy Idea	Holy Transparency, Holy Omniscience
Affirmation	Love is the coherence that holds everything together
Belief	I believe there is divine truth in silence, there is love in the unknown.
Confession	I am rooted in mystery.

Fives are known for acceptance, mindful silence, and allowing all facts, answers, theories, and mysteries to exist together. Setting aside the forceful need to discern every point of data allows for transparent acceptance and compassionate coherence. With this posture of the mind, love is no longer anonymous or distant, but experientially known—received, though not utterly known. [page 136]

"Not needing to know everything is the only
thing one needs to know." [page 137]

Type Six

Traditional Holy Idea	Holy Faith, Holy Strength
Affirmation	I am courageous because of love.
Belief	I believe there is divine love grounded in compassion that liberates fear.
Confession	I make an option for the absurd to believe beyond belief.

Doubt isn't the opposite of faith; certainty is. Courage is being honest with fear, facing the illusions and truths fear conceals. In a pseudo-spiritual trust fall, the divine mind of Sixes finds authentic peace through liberating their concerns by putting on their courage—seemingly the most absurd option they can make. [page 137]

"Faith is courageous doubt." [page 137]

Type Seven

Traditional Holy Idea	Holy Wisdom, Holy Work, Holy Plan
Affirmation	In the present I am loved.
Belief	I believe constancy through constraint leads to contentment.
Confession	I affirm the enoughness of each moment.

Sevens cannot participate in the present while fixated on anticipating the future. The Holy Truth invites Sevens to slow down the speed of their minds long enough to remember that the present moment is always enough. The Seven's divine thought celebrates constancy through constraint, even as it fosters spiritual flourishing. [page 138]

"This moment, *now*, is the only moment that matters." [page 138]

Type Eight

Traditional Holy Idea	Holy Truth
Affirmation	I am held in compassionate love.
Belief	I believe all truth comes from the source of love.
Confession	I willingly surrender to love.

Love is truth made vulnerable and rejection is a likely factor in any exchange of love. Opening oneself in love to the possibility of rejection is true strength. The divine mind of the Eights open their heart, inviting them to bear their most woundable and tender selves as the validation of their power, reconciling their powerlessness though submission. [page 139]

> "Bearing their most woundable and tender selves is the validation of their power." [page 139]

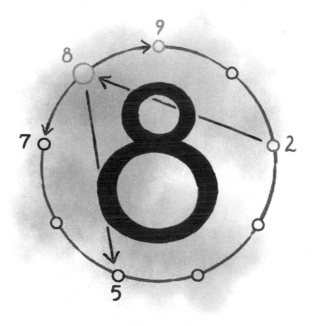

Type Nine

Traditional Holy Idea	Holy Love
Affirmation	I cooperate with love.
Belief	I believe love anchors my being in compassionate self-awareness.
Confession	I am a source of love because I first love myself.

Nines know that to love is to be love. At the top of the Enneagram, Nines permeate the world with love from the clarity of their minds. But to diminish the outreach of love—even to oneself—is to reduce its Essence. To be love is to start by loving oneself without condition, commentary, or constraint. [page 140]

"The experience of love has to be an internalized one." [page140]

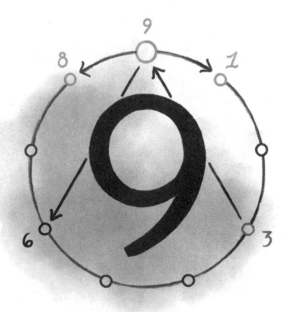

- When we are habitually entrenched in our Passions and Fixations, the concept of our Holy Idea can stir up resistance or disbelief within us. Sometimes our bodies reveal this tension in a tightening of the shoulders, a grinding of the jaw, or guardedly crossing arms or legs. What thoughts and feelings and physical sensations did you experience while reading how your type affirms its Holy Idea?

  _____

  _____

  _____

  _____

  _____

- Consider when you woke up this morning. What was the first "truth" you told yourself? Was it condemning, or was it compassionate?

  _____

  _____

  _____

  _____

- What would it look like for you to allow space for your Holy Idea daily? How would it shift your mental dialogue and daily decisions?

  _____

  _____

  _____

  _____

  _____

- How would it shift the way you engage your relationships?

  _____

  _____

  _____

  _____

- How would it shift your spiritual life?

_____

_____

_____

_____

_____

- Embracing your type's Holy Idea is an ongoing, intentional journey. How might you create space in your weekly and daily schedule to attend to this process?

_____

_____

_____

_____

_____

- Based on what you know about yourself and your type, what challenges do you foresee in embracing your Holy Idea—in feelings, thought, lifestyle, relationships, schedule, and general focus?

_____

_____

_____

_____

_____

Invitation

HOLY IDEA CENTERING PRACTICE

Centering Prayer is a contemplative practice that prepares us to receive the gift of experiencing the Divine's presence with us. Centering Prayer is grounded in love and is a practice that allows us to receive the divine belonging we are all invited into. This kind of intentional prayer is proven to increase mental, emotional, and physical well-being when practiced for twenty minutes, two times a day. But any amount of time spent in spiritual connection with the love that offers us belonging is never wasted. As with all new practices, it's wise to start out slowly. To start this practice, set a timer for five to ten minutes of prayer at first.

1. Sit in an upright, attentive posture which allows for an erect spine (as you are able) and an open heart. Place your hands in your lap, palms and fingers relaxed.
2. With eyes closed, direct your attention to the presence of God. Yield your focus, your whole self, to the Divine.
3. In your mind, recite your type's Holy Idea confession. Let it settle in your mind, heart, and body. Continue holding your confession in mind, allowing your focus to settle on each word as you repeat your prayer.
4. Whenever you notice your thoughts wandering, gently return your attention to your confession.
5. As your prayer time comes to an end, allow yourself to transition to your active life with gentleness and grace.

FIXATIONS

Holy Ideas are the truths that bring clarity to our consciousness and our view on reality, while Fixations keep us stuck in our old pattern of behavior. Holy Ideas and Fixations are the two sides of the coin our Head Center flips over and over and over again. If the Holy Idea is the first truth we tell ourselves, then the Fixation is the original lie that keeps us trapped in an illusion. Our Fixation is the learned mental justification for remaining disconnected from our Essence. [page 142]

"The move from fixated to free is our path to ultimate liberation." [page 142]

When our Kidlife Crisis set in and dimmed the light of our Holy Idea, we turned to something else to guide us, our Fixations. Eventually, we realize that we no longer control our Fixations, rather they control us—creating pain and loss in our lives, relationships, and communities. [page 146] Though we may be repulsed by the unbecoming expressions of our personalities, the truth is that we created them out of a very real need. Rather than resisting our Fixations, which only makes them stronger, the path to liberation is found when we learn to make room for them in the interior landscape of our lives. Why? Because when we observe them rather than ignore them, we learn to recognize when we start slipping into self-sabotaging patterns.

FIXATIONS BY TYPE

Type One	Resentment
Type Two	Flattery
Type Three	Vanity
Type Four	Melancholy
Type Five	Stinginess
Type Six	Cowardice
Type Seven	Planning
Type Eight	Vengeance
Type Nine	Indolence

Type One: *Resentment*

Those dominant in type One are preoccupied with structure, order, good vs. bad, right vs. wrong, which is based on their Basic Fear of being corrupt and beyond redemption. This leads to resentment levied at themselves for knowing how they ought to live yet still failing to comply with their standards of perfection. [page 150]

Type Two: *Flattery*

Twos are primarily concerned with being a source of nurturing care in their world which leads to their preoccupation with heart to heart connections. When their relationships don't go the way they hoped, they look inward and flatter themselves by assuming they are solely responsible for the health and depth of the connection. [page 151]

Type Three: *Vanity*

Threes are caught on a hamster wheel of trying to earn their intrinsic value. Winning success and status symbols aren't the point, it's just the easiest way to earn the validation they fear they've lost. And when they win, their vanity enables them to convince themselves that they actually earned love. [page 152]

Type Four: *Melancholy*

Those dominant in type Four are generally obsessed with the authentic beauty of everything. But they are caught by the pain of never being able to materialize the ideal and beautiful things they imagine. Fours internalize this pain and allow the melancholy to shape the way they see the world. [page 153]

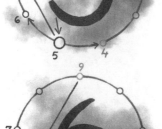

Type Five: *Stinginess*

Fives are preoccupied with uncertainty and obsessed with finding solutions, analyzing threats, and reframing questions as an attempt to display love. In social settings, this comes across as stinginess or retention. Ironically, this preoccupation keeps them distracted from meaningful mental pursuits and realizing the Holy Idea of transparency. [page 154]

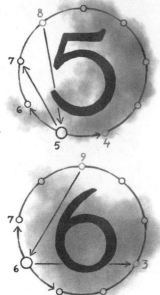

Type Six: *Cowardice*

Those dominant in type Six are preoccupied with threat forecasting as a way of caring for those in their social circles. Whether they avoid possible threats or take them head on, either path is racked with self-doubt, further bracing the cowardice complex which keeps them second guessing their innate courage. [page 154]

Type Seven: *Planning*

Sevens are preoccupied with preoccupation; obsessively chasing what they can consume—be it experiences, relationships, or knowledge. On the run from their Basic Fear of being trapped in the pain of their hearts, the Sevens' Fixation of planning and anticipating always leaves them empty and unsatisfied. [page 155]

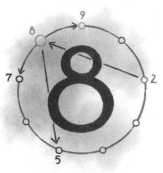

Type Eight: *Vengeance*

Rather than being honest with their feelings, Eights catalyze them into an externalized projection of control. This preoccupation with control plays out in avoiding being taken advantage of, betrayed, or harmed through preemptively fighting back with any perceived threat, which then leads Eights to vengeance—beating themselves up for the too-muchness of how they show up in the world. [page 155]

Type Nine: *Indolence*

Nines desire uninterrupted interior harmony and they will do nearly anything to avoid disturbance. This preoccupation with avoidance leads to a listless obsession with remaining unbothered by not bothering their environment. Ironically, Nines so often end up feeling exhausted from the constant effort of avoiding external efforts. [page 156]

- Our Fixations shape our lives, relationships, and mindsets in unique ways. Reflect on what this looks like for you.

_____

_____

_____

_____

_____

- In what way does your Fixation play in your head as a preoccupation, obsession, and complex? [page 148–150]

_____

_____

_____

_____

_____

- We created our Fixations to serve an internal need. What does your experience of your Fixation reveal to you about what you need, what you long for?

_____

_____

_____

_____

_____

- How does your Fixation get in the way of your decisions, relationships, emotional wellbeing, and work?

_____

_____

_____

_____

- How does your Fixation keep you disconnected from your true Essence?

_____

_____

_____

_____

- On page 149, we learned how Fixations create neuro-grooves of automatic thought and behavior in our minds. What are the internal messages and habits that your Fixation has prompted in your mind? How do you think you might go about checking these misinformed mindsets?

_____

_____

_____

_____

HUMILITY AND HUMOR

Awareness of our Fixation won't remove it from us. And remember, this journey is about belonging, so even these less-flattering parts of ourselves belong.

Father Richard Rohr says that until we've done our shadow work, the patient work of making peace with our Fixations, we probably won't have a sense of humor about ourselves. So when we find ourselves falling back into old patterns, addictions, or harmful behaviors, we have to be able to laugh at ourselves as one of the ways of disarming our tendencies. When we find the humor of these predictable patterns in our lives, we unlock one more way to humbly receive the gift of our humanity, and humility is the door we pass through to enter the welcoming presence of divine love. [page 68]

> "We carry within us more promise and potential than we could desire.
> And we are loved more than we want to be loved." [page 167]

- Sometimes we let our Fixations take the driver's seat in our lives. What signs and symptoms show up when your Fixation has taken over?

_____

_____

_____

_____

_____

_____

- Consider your personal stance toward humility. Is this something you value? Why or why not?

_____

_____

_____

_____

_____

- What role does humility play in your relationship with yourself and with others?

_____

_____

_____

_____

_____

- In what ways might you be able to cultivate a sense of humor about yourself?

_____

_____

_____

_____

_____

REFLECTION OR DISCUSSION QUESTION

- When we resist practicing humility in life, it's often an instinctual attempt at protecting ourselves from losing something—like, losing respect, risking social standing, or being misunderstood. What fear seems to block you the most from practicing humility at the workplace, at home, at social gatherings, and in your spiritual life? How might we be able to foster a humble and gracious atmosphere for ourselves and others?

_____

_____

_____

_____

_____

_____

_____

_____

_____

_____

Invitation

LOVING KINDNESS MEDITATION

The Loving Kindness meditation is a practice that develops radical compassion for yourself and others. Called metta bhavana in the Buddhist tradition, though it may be adapted or used more broadly, this practice allows us to form greater awareness of our own belovedness and dials down the voice of our inner critic. After falling into a natural cadence with these lines and owning them as self-intentions we can include others in successive stages: (1) those who love me, (2) those I love, (3) those who are difficult for me, and (4) those in my larger community.

The full benefit is experienced when this practice spans 15–20 minutes, with a few minutes for each successive stage. But you can adjust the time according to your time constraints. The important part is to use the practice.

SUGGESTED TYPE-SPECIFIC MEDITATIONS

Type One	Type Four	Type Seven
May I be at ease	May I see myself	May I be free
May I breathe peacefully	May I know myself	May I be content
May I find freedom in rest	May I love myself	May I rest in this moment
Type Two	**Type Five**	**Type Eight**
May I offer love	May I be here now	May I be openhearted
May I receive love	May I say yes to silence	May I be loving
May I love myself	May I let go	May I be vulnerable
Type Three	**Type Six**	**Type Nine**
May I own my worth	May I embrace my fears	May I be present
May I own my value	May I embrace my faith	May I own my power
May I be embraced by love	May I embrace my courage	May I have inner peace

To Start the Loving Kindness Meditation:

1. Choose three affirming statements or phrases that attend to a tender part of your heart, or select your type's suggested mantra from the chart above.

2. Determine who you want to include in this practice, the people and groups you hope will also benefit from your mindful loving kindness.

3. Assume a posture that is both relaxed and attentive. Close your eyes or allow your gaze to gently drift to the floor 2–3 feet in front of you. Draw attention to your breathing and allow it to return you to the present moment every time you get distracted.

4. For 3–4 minutes, repeat your affirming phrases to yourself. Then, call to mind the next person(s) you want to include, and repeat the phrase for them for 3–4 minutes. Continue through the stages until you've finished.

— 4 —

The Enneagram of Belonging: Chapters 8–9

Belonging for the Heart

Moving from the hard work of self-observation to the compassionate work of self-remembering leads us to the thrilling work of living into the gift of our freedom. But this is harder than we realize because many of us suffer from a spiritual and personal fear of heights. It's like we only allow ourselves so much growth before we allow our inner critic to roll out the highlight reel of our subconscious imposter syndrome.

We all seem to get stuck at a comfortable psycho-spiritual set point that keeps us from growing. And it's daunting to shake up this set-point, because it requires much of us. [page 176]

- How do you experience your own attempts at self-limiting? In what ways have you cautiously held yourself back from growth? Reflect on what fear you hold behind this behavior.

_____

_____

_____

_____

_____

- In what ways have you allowed yourself to stay tethered to your Fixation and personal baggage, and why?

  _____

  _____

  _____

  _____

  _____

- What underlying fears do you carry with you about the practices of prayer and meditation and the process of belonging?

  _____

  _____

  _____

  _____

  _____

- In reading the moving story of forgiveness and acceptance from *The Mission* on pages 178–179, what internal fragments in your own life does this story prompt you to embrace?

  _____

  _____

  _____

  _____

  _____

  _____

VIRTUES

Just like Fixations and Holy Ideas are the two sides of the coin our mind flips, Virtues and Passions are the two sides of the coin our heart flips over and over. Virtues are the deepest, truest part of our hearts that were disconnected as a result of our Kidlife Crisis. They are the gift of the heart centered in the reality of radical love. And they are what can form us into the forces of love the world so needs today. [page 181]

Head Center	Heart Center
Holy Idea	Virtue
Fixation	Passion

The partnership between our Holy Ideas and our Virtues is where we connect with our true Essence. [page 181]

VIRTUES

VIRTUES ACCORDING TO TYPE

Type One	Serenity	Ones live into the virtue of Serenity when they internalize the message that their flaws are what make them perfectly beautiful.
Type Two	Humility	For the Two, living into the virtue of humility is a return to the unpretentious ownership of all that is fabulous about themselves.
Type Three	Authenticity	Threes living into the virtue of authenticity is an acceptance that they were always loved, and that being loved is the most truthful way of being themselves.

(cont.)

Type Four	Equanimity	For the Four to return to the Virtue of equanimity, their gift to stay grounded and present even while their interior lives are tossed are tossed to the extremes.
Type Five	Nonattachment	Fives live into nonattachment when they cultivate a posture of open-handedness with all that they've uncovered in their mental pursuits, rather than hoarding it for themselves.
Type Six	Courage	Sixes live into the Virtue of courage when they disempower fearful lies by returning to the truth that they will not be overcome by fear.
Type Seven	Sobriety	For the Seven, sobriety is returning to what feels unsatisfied in their hearts and letting it guide them into the enoughness of every moment.
Type Eight	Innocence	Eights who return to their Virtue when they remember that their inner innocence is the deepest, strongest source of their power.
Type Nine	Action	Nines wake up to their Virtue when they fully live their reality and put love in action, both for themselves as well as others.

[pages 182–184]

> "Even if we can't fully own the goodness within us,
> we somehow know it's true." [page 188]

When we can allow our Virtue to take the lead in what guides our sense of being, we begin to experience how the Enneagram supports flourishing in our relationships, community, friendships, and ultimately how we live faithfully into our vocational commitments. [page 184] It's our Virtues that will heal the world and this healing starts inside each of us, opening our hearts to our whole selves so that when confronted with human need, injustice, and the opportunity to be generous, we are able to be of service and allow ourselves to be saved. [page 189]

No one else can help us locate or live into our Virtue. We get to find it for ourselves. And contemplative practice is one such way of accessing the gifts of our Virtues. In solitude, silence, and stillness the qualities of our Virtue are remembered and fully received. [page 188] Contemplative practice enables us to discover our own belovedness and to perceive the belovedness of others. And loving ourselves makes room for us to be a force of love in the world. [page 189]

To learn contemplative practices for solitude, silence, and stillness, refer to *The Sacred Enneagram Workbook*, also by Christopher L. Heuertz.

- How do you currently find space for solitude, silence, and stillness in your daily life?

_____

_____

_____

_____

- Like Mother Teresa's noisy yet sacred chapel [page 187], how might you create more opportunities to show up for solitude, silence, and stillness in between the hustle and bustle of everyday living?

_____

_____

_____

_____

- Based on what you understand about yourself and your type, what challenges—current or potential—do you face in connecting with your Virtue through solitude, silence, and stillness?

_____

_____

_____

_____

Reflect on the story of the Sadhu on pages 189–190. How might the struggles and challenges you face in learning to live into your Virtue actually be the path to saving your own life? How might they pave the way to compassion?

> "What we are looking for has always been as
> close to us as our hearts." [page 188]

PASSIONS

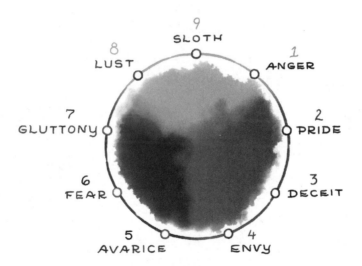

The Passions are the emotional coping skills of each type. The counterpoint to Virtues, the Passions are how our hearts ache and long to reconnect with our lost Essence. It's our souls' clarion call to return home. [pages 194–195]

When our Basic Fear arises in us, our Passions automatically step in to contend with our fear. Just like Fixations are the mental justification for remaining disconnected from our Essence, Passions are the emotional justification of our heart for remaining disconnected from our true self. Like a child who hasn't been given an adequate amount of security and control over their circumstances, our inner child utilizes our Fixations and Passions to get happiness. [page 196] But all of this is a subconscious behavioral system; we really don't know what we're doing. So, as we awaken to our Passions and the role they play in our lives, let's approach this part of the journey with compassion and understanding.

The Passion for each type may manifest in one of two ways: Passion and Counterpassion. Living out of our Counterpassion feels like growth. But in reality, it is a self-delusional workaround for true emotional, mental, and spiritual growth. [pages 198–199]

Another dynamic exists within the Passions: the Inner Polarities, which represent the two inner behavioral postures each of us vacillate between. [page 203]

Type	Traditional Passion	Counterpassion	Description	Inner Polarity
One	Anger	Renouncement	Ones can swing from renouncement to tolerant acquiescence, enabling them to maintain a muted internal frustration and a delusional sense of moral superiority.	Security ←→ Sensitivity
Two	Pride	Self-Effacement	Twos who don't face their pride express their counterpassion through false humility, making them feel less important and the inner strength of their own Virtue of true humility.	Freedom ←→ Intimacy
Three	Deceit	Self-Restraint	Threes unaware of their tendency to downplay their worth reach for self-restraint, still a tactic to manage the perceptions of others.	Depersonalization ←→ Self-Interest
Four	Envy	Self-Sufficiency	Fours swing from the pain of their envy to the convincing belief that they don't need anyone or anything, which reinforces the narrative of abandonment.	Disorientation ←→ Vindication

(cont.)

Type	Traditional Passion	Counterpassion	Description	Inner Polarity
Five	Avarice	Extravagance	Fives form a sense of generosity with gifts and information as a way to control resources they still quietly withhold.	Distrust ←→ Certitude
Six	Fear	Temerity	Sixes counter their fear with boldness which looks like courage but is really compensating for veiled fear.	Attack ←→ Surrender
Seven	Gluttony	Austerity	Sevens who exhaust all options swing to self-control as a way to dial-in and refocus their search for distraction.	Impermanence ←→ Sacrifice
Eight	Lust	Wariness	Eights turn from intense control to intense caution, a measured restraint that is still fueled by control.	Submission ←→ Supremacy
Nine	Sloth	Hyperactivity	Nines who experience unintended consequences of their slothfulness swing to hyperactivity, but which still aimed at self-perfection, rather than self-love.	Lethargy ←→ Hyperactivity

- How would you describe your relationship with your Passion?

  _____

  _____

  _____

  _____

- How has your Passion expressed itself throughout your lifetime?

  _____

  _____

  _____

  _____

• How has your counterpassion shown up in your life?

_____

_____

_____

_____

_____

_____

• Taking a look at your type's inner polarity, how have you seen this dynamic shape your emotions and sense of well-being?

_____

_____

_____

_____

_____

_____

The Counters of Passion Theory

The Passions, as they've been taught traditionally, are helpful, but they do not form a comprehensive theory for the complex subconscious strategies we use to make up for our loss of belonging.

The Counters of Passions is a detailed framework for understanding the way our Passions attempt to get us, if not home, at least somewhere safe. It's important to note that the Counters of Passion compassionately reframe the Passions not as sins, as they have been taught, but as misled and sometimes addictive attempts to make up for the loss of belonging we all suffer. [page 211]

The Intelligence Centers form our views of reality and we find the Passions are expressed in a unique way through each center, like the same picture viewed through different lenses. These expressions are carnal hunger held in the Body Center, an emotional ache held in the Heart Center, and the existential restlessness held in the Head Center. [page 213]

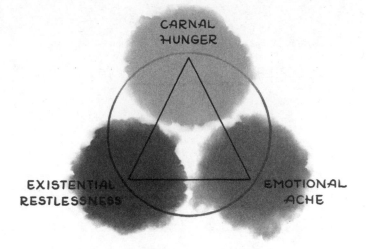

For each type, our Passion is primarily experienced in our dominant Intelligence Center. Our Passion hides in our repressed Intelligence Center, the most unconscious part of our perception. The repressed center then serves as an incubator, strengthening our Passion's hold on us.

The challenge is to learn to recognize how we experience our Passion in each of our Centers so that when one driving force takes over, the other two can hold it accountable. [page 214]

Overlaying the nine traditional Passions of the Enneagram with each Intelligence Center offers accuracy, clarity, and candor. If we can truthfully admit to ourselves what we're contending with, then we know how to face, accept, and make peace with the sometimes painful layers of the Enneagram's Passions. [page 214]

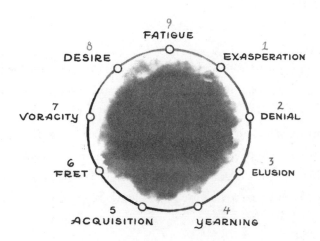

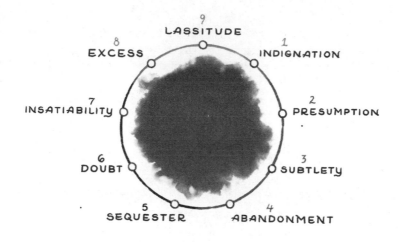

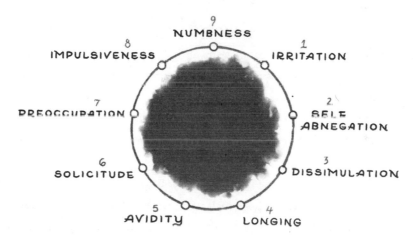

Counters of the Passions by Type

TYPE ONE

Traditional Passion	Carnal Hunger	Emotional Ache	Existential Restlessness
Anger	Exasperation	Indignation	Irritation

Ones carry an exhausting *exasperation* in their bodies. When combined with the emotion of *indignation*, Ones' idealism turns in on themselves, creating deep and sometimes physical pain. Having repressed their Head Center, this exasperated indignation leads to a persistent mental irritability, sometimes coming out as anger. [pages 215–216]

TYPE TWO

Traditional Passion	Carnal Hunger	Emotional Ache	Existential Restlessness
Pride	Denial	Presumption	Self-Abnegation

Twos' *denial* of their own needs is held in their body, yet they can't help but crave that these desires be met. This leads to passive-aggressive presumption that others would return what they offer of themselves. Presuming is also hidden in the assumption that if they did make their needs known, they would only experience rejection. *Self-abnegation* is the mental argument to give away more of themselves at their own expense. [page 217]

TYPE THREE

Traditional Passion	Carnal Hunger	Emotional Ache	Existential Restlessness
Deceit	Elusion	Subtlety	Dissimulation

Threes' preoccupation with authenticity fortifies an internal pendulum which swings between deception and integrity. Threes handle this ever-present duplicity in their bodies by avoiding it, but evading their inner deception merely serves to give it more power. Aching from this disconnect, Threes' repressed Heart Center can't bear to face yet another inner imperfection, so they turn to over- or underexaggerating themselves socially. In this way, Threes hope to be seen as more legitimate than they really are, even as they disguise what they won't or can't be truthful about. [pages 217–218]

TYPE FOUR

Traditional Passion	Carnal Hunger	Emotional Ache	Existential Restlessness
Envy	Yearning	Abandonment	Longing

Fours experience envy as a strong yearning held in their bodies. In repressing their Body Center, this yearning is suppressed by their abandoned heart's sense, lest it becomes too strong of an internal driver. Fours translate the world through an emotional sense of abandonment—both self-abandonment and their unconscious attempts to be or feel abandoned by others. This is the gentler side of their longing for what they perceive to be more significant than the quality of their reality. [pages 218–219]

TYPE FIVE

Traditional Passion	Carnal Hunger	Emotional Ache	Existential Restlessness
Avarice	Acquisition	Sequester	Avidity

Fives' voracious need to *acquire* analysis, questions, and research is a substitute for physical hunger felt in their bodies. Having repressed their Body Center, this acquisitive hunger supports the sequestering of the Fives' heart by their mind—the handing over of their seemingly distrustful emotions to their mental faculties. With sequestered hearts, their self-isolating tendency is given over to an eagerness to consume and connect all things. [pages 219–220]

TYPE SIX

Traditional Passion	Carnal Hunger	Emotional Ache	Existential Restlessness
Fear	Fret	Questioning Doubt	Solicitude

The burden of constantly forecasting potential threats is carried in the bodies of Sixes. They experience a physical pull in two directions: *suspicion* for all that is minutely off, and a visceral sense of *fret*. The pain of all this gets parked in the Heart Center. Sixes' compulsion for *self-doubt* combined with their repressed Head Center, leads to the uneasiness of their anxious minds. [page 220]

TYPE SEVEN

Traditional Passion	Carnal Hunger	Emotional Ache	Existential Restlessness
Gluttony	Voracity	Insatiability	Preoccupation

The Seven's gluttony is a compulsion of overconsuming pleasurable options as a distraction from facing inner pain or suffering. This voracious appetite triggers the idealization of insatiability which characterizes the Seven's emotional ache. Their repressed Heart Center fuels this dissatisfaction with no way to check it. Yet, savvy problem solvers, the Sevens remain preoccupied, immersed in the daydream of anticipating what will feed their consumption next. [page 221]

TYPE EIGHT

Traditional Passion	Carnal Hunger	Emotional Ache	Existential Restlessness
Lust	Desire	Excess	Impulsiveness

Eights experience their Passion as a physical intensity for *desire* that grows within, fueled by the frustration of its too-muchness. Having repressed their Heart Center, this desire is often isolated from the whole and unaccountable in its *excessiveness* or the surplus of energy it produces. Though Eights are quick-thinking, their *impulsive* lack of reasoning gives more power to their Passion, creating the quandaries many Eights manufacture for themselves and others. [pages 221–222]

TYPE NINE

Traditional Passion	Carnal Hunger	Emotional Ache	Existential Restlessness
Sloth	Fatigue	Lassitude	Numbness

Often misunderstood as complacent (as if Nines are pleased with themselves) or apathetic, Nines quickly become worn out from projecting the inner peace they long for internally. With forgotten Body Centers, Nines' exhaustion leads to physical fatigue and an emotional lethargy that takes over their hearts. To cope with all that overwhelms them, Nines turn their minds over to a state of numbness. [page 222–223]

With a compassionate lens, we can appreciate how very difficult it is to be each of us. In our pursuit of wholeness, the Passions are our unlikely friend. And if we can lean into deeper awareness of our self-defeating patterns, we can all the more empower ourselves to course-correct. [page 224]

> "Even our Passions belong. When we recognize this and seek to learn from our Passions instead of living in denial of them, we can press deeper into the journey of returning to our true selves." [page 224]

- How does your Passion tell you about the innocent desires and fears you carry in your true Essence?

_____

_____

_____

_____

_____

- How does the inner process of your Passion cloud your experience and understanding of divine love and grace?

_____

_____

_____

_____

_____

- Reflect on recent times when your Passion was strongly triggered. What set it in motion?

_____

_____

_____

_____

_____

- How did the automatic response of your Passion influence your mood, mental clarity, and relationships?

_____

_____

_____

_____

- What practical thing can you do to strengthen your awareness of your Passion and the inner needs it attempts to compensate for?

  _____

  _____

  _____

  _____

  _____

- The Enneagram shows us that resisting and denying our Passions further only strengthens them. What practical gesture of acceptance might you do next time to interrupt your triggered Passion's cycle?

  _____

  _____

  _____

  _____

  _____

REFLECTION OR DISCUSSION QUESTION

- Many of us grew up thinking desires and Passions were at best indulgent, and at worst, sinful. Reflect on the truth that each and every one of us has an innate yearning (Passion) to receive a particular gift from the world, and an innate gift (Virtue) to give the world. What does it tell you about our collective humanity? How can we cultivate more space for both gifts and needs for ourselves and for the people in our social circles?

  _____

  _____

  _____

  _____

The Enneagram of Belonging: Chapter 10

Belonging for the Body

So far, we have journeyed from our Head Center in the conscious level, to our Heart Center in the subconscious level. And now we turn to complete the journey to the Body Center at the unconscious level. Here we find the three Instincts: Self-Preservation, Sexual, and Social. These Instincts are very powerful and quite possibly the most impactful aspect of what shapes our type, yet almost completely unobserved—driving our behavior at a level deeper than our awareness. [pages 227–229]

Fixations & Holy Ideas	Head Center	Conscious Level
Passions & Virtues	Heart Center	Subconscious Level
Subtypes	Body Center	Unconscious Level

Here the Enneagram helps us dive into understanding our instinctual compulsions and addictive patterns. Left unchecked, these compulsions and patterns create our most serious personal, mental, emotional, spiritual, and communal obstacles to belonging. [pages 270–271]

Though Instincts don't have the final word on how we present personality, they create the brain chemistry which builds the rails our personality moves along. They also explain how individuals with the same type can be so different from each other. [page 228]

> "Though typically under-examined, our Instincts may be the most impacting aspect of what shapes our type." [page 231]

This leg of the journey is an invitation to discover what somatic intelligence has to teach us. Because this intelligence is stored away deep in our unconscious, it takes a kind of attunement that most of us have yet to develop. It may be difficult, but it is not impossible. [page 231]

- Self-Preservation Instinct: our compulsion for survival on a very practical level, our inherent instinct to do what we can to ensure that we, and those we love, are going to be okay.
- Sexual Instinct: the part of our physiology that is energized by its zest for life, which can show up as directed toward a person we are attracted to or, more broadly, toward a creative or intellectual undertaking.
- Social Instinct: the part of our unconscious that finds safety, support, and identity in group affiliation.

Each Intelligence Center is preoccupied with a specific desire. In the Body Center: Eight, Nine, and One are focused on control. In the Heart Center: Two, Three, and Four are focused on making connections. And in the Head Center: Five, Six, and Seven are focused on maintaining concern for security and stability.

Your Intelligence Center does not determine your Instinct, but it does shape the focus of your Instinct. For example, a type Eight (Body Center) with a repressed Heart Center can lead with a Social Instinct, which allows for reconnection with heart. But the Instinct is still expressed as the Body Center's preoccupation with control. [pages 250–251]

Like other repeating fractals within the Enneagram, each Instinct is expressed in three different ways as they relate to each Intelligence Center.

The Self-Preservation Instinct for Regulation is Body Centered Intelligence
   for Control
The Self-Preservation Instinct for Preparation is Heart Intelligence for Connection
The Self-Preservation Instinct for Subsistence is Head Intelligence for Concern
The Sexual Instinct for Enticement is Body Intelligence for Control
The Sexual Instinct for Exploration is Heart Intelligence for Connection
The Sexual Instinct for Opportunity is Head Intelligence for Concern
The Social Instinct for Dominance is Body Intelligence for Control
The Social Instinct for Association is Heart Intelligence for Connection
The Social Instinct for Cooperation is Head Intelligence for Concern

[pages 249–250]

Self-Preservation for Regulation at Work in the Body Center

The basis for the Self-Preservation Instinct is the fundamental practice of self-care. Self-Preservation people generally need to ensure they've gotten enough sleep, exercising consistently, and committing to a diet that serves their sense of well-being. Additionally, they tend to find practical ways of making sure their mental, emotional, biological, and spiritual needs are met. Now this doesn't imply that these needs are met through self-reflection, rather more often they are responding to the unconscious drive. [pages 236–237]

Self-Preservation Preparation at Work in the Heart Center

The second expression of Self-Preservation arises from the Heart Center and presents as preparation. Sometimes referred to as a nesting instinct or a bias for domesticity or home-making, this Instinct leads the individual to create a safe, clean, and comfortable home because in all life there is a preparation aspect to making home not only a safe place for us, but also for those we welcome into it. [page 238]

Self-Preservation for Subsistence at Work in the Head Center

The third expression seeks to ensure subsistence and sustaining our own sense of control, connection, and those things we're most concerned about. The instinct is the lingering drive in all of us to store up for the future, saving for our retirement, making sure we'll have enough to continue living the way we want and need to live, and ensuring the comfort and safety of those we love. [page 239–240]

And just as we all have instincts to preserve our life, we also have inherent drives to expand our life. Let's turn now to the Sexual Instinct. [page 240]

Sexual Enticement at Work in the Body Center

The first aspect of the Sexual Instinct is the basic drive for sex. While more nuanced and complex in humans than in animals, this enticing aspect of the Sexual Instinct is just as present even if way less consciously observed. We see this in subtle social cues online and face-to-face as individuals put themselves out into the world through instinctual hints to see what responses will come back—much like echolocation. [pages 241–242]

Sexual Exploration at Work in the Heart Center

Sexual Exploration is centered in the heart as an unconscious way of scoping possibilities for intimate connection. There's a purely animal instinct in all of us that searches for connections and investigates messages that might have been left for us. This form of Sexual Instinct prompts many of us to be alert and looking to connect with others. [page 242]

Sexual Opportunity at Work in the Head Center

The third expression of the Sexual Instinct is focused on the prospect for opportunity. There's an unconscious compulsion and willingness to risk discomfort or even pain in order to expand our lives with a promising opportunity. It's where the mere possibility of a thing is more exciting than actually seizing whatever one is chasing after. This instinct is what prompts many of us to try different things and explore new places. [page 243]

Traditionally, the Social Instinct has to do with belonging. But the complexities of belonging show up in three distinct ways. [page 244]

Social Dominance at Work in the Body Center

On a gut level, the Social Instinct is expressed in how we navigate the various power dynamics at play in our social interactions. This Social Instinct in all of us shows up in the ways we adjust to the alpha or how we handle unspoken power dynamics in every social circle. With it, we intuit who to trust, when to submit, and when to fight and protect. [page 245]

Social Instinct for Association at Work in the Heart Center

The Social Instinct for group association shows up in several ways—belonging to our neighborhood association, or our worshiping community, or even a club with a shared interest. This doesn't require *intimate* connections, rather it's focused on group identity. Being a part of groups meets an unconscious need for association and belonging. [page 246]

Social Cooperation at Work in the Head Center

Finally, the Social Instinct is expressed in our drive for cooperation and the practical betterment of the group(s) we're a part of. It shows up in the natural affinity we all have to know how to help one another and build a better world. This instinct prompts a response to suffering or injustice. [page 247–248]

> "Our Instincts are our bodies somatic impulses for survival." [page 250]

Intelligence Center	Instinct	Concentration	8-9-1 Focus	2-3-4 Focus	5-6-7 Focus
Body Intelligence	Self-Preservation Instinct	Regulation	Control	Connection	Concern
Body Intelligence	Sexual Instinct	Enticement	Control	Connection	Concern
Body Intelligence	Social Instinct	Dominance	Control	Connection	Concern
Heart Intelligence	Self-Preservation Instinct	Preparation	Control	Connection	Concern
Heart Intelligence	Sexual Instinct	Exploration	Control	Connection	Concern
Heart Intelligence	Social Instinct	Cooperation	Control	Connection	Concern
Head Intelligence	Self-Preservation Instinct	Subsistence	Control	Connection	Concern
Head Intelligence	Sexual Instinct	Opportunity	Control	Connection	Concern
Head Intelligence	Social Instinct	Association	Control	Connection	Concern

[page 252]

- Of the three Instincts, which one do you recognize the most in yourself? Which Instinct would you rank second and third?

_____

_____

_____

_____

_____

- Write a few examples of how the Self-Preservation Instinct shows up in your life.

_____

_____

_____

_____

_____

- Write a few examples of how the Sexual Instinct shows up in your life.

_____

_____

_____

_____

_____

- Write a few examples of how the Social Instinct shows up in your life.

_____

_____

_____

_____

- In what ways have you experienced your type's Focus shape the direction of your attention and energy?

_____

_____

_____

_____

Now that we've learned how the Instincts are expressed through the Intelligence Centers, let's consider how they shape each Enneagram type into Subtypes. The Subtypes explain the three different shades within each type, identifying a total of twenty-seven Subtypes. [page 253]

Similar to the interplay of the Intelligence Centers, each of the twenty-seven Subtypes are led by a dominant Instinct.

Let's remember that each type also includes a Countertype, called out in the chart below. For Countertypes, the Instinct makes a counter move against the type's Passion, almost as if the Instinct considers the Passion as something that can't or shouldn't be permissible. [page 255]

THE TWENTY-SEVEN SUBTYPES

Self-Preservation One	Worry

The most compassionate of Ones because of their controlled presence, but inwardly they are incredibly hard on themselves and attuned to anger.

Sexual One (Countertype)	Zeal

Project their inner drive for perfection on those closest to them; more comfortable expressing anger; most assertive and determined to carry out their standard of goodness.

Social One	Non-Adaptability

Embody their vision for excellence through deep convictions; their commitment can be intimidating; believe they know the only way to heal the world and can self-isolate.

Self-Preservation Two (Countertype)	Privilege

Project a childlike innocence; their natural ability to care for others can be a subconscious attempt to meet their needs, leading to a trade of sorts; the most heart-reserved of Twos.

Sexual Two	Aggression

Captivating and sometimes intrusive presence attracts attention; determined and strong-willed; make thoughtful sacrifices to ensure the connections they want; highly persuasive.

Social Two	Ambition

Strategic about making presence and accomplishments known; support people they value; broker connections; project strong and inspiring presence aligned with important efforts.

Self-Preservation Three (Countertype)	Security

Hard work ethic and dedication to excellence; reliable and faithful to commitments; project low-key nature and understate their need for gratitude; boundaries are important to them.

Sexual Three	Femininity/Masculinity

Emphasize image and being perceived as desirable; add value to earn value; invest in small groups and individuals; can present as coy and demure; present a positive presence.

Social Three	Prestige

Gravitate toward the center of attention; focused on being seen as successful and significant; build notable reputation; highly confident and sensitive to critique; competitive.

Self-Preservation Four (Countertype)	Tenacity

Positive curiosity; downplay inner pain; believe the value of their emotional acuity is resilience; hold self to high standards; focus on helping others; private but not withdrawn.

Sexual Four	Competition

Intense and competitive presence; work to ensure needs are satisfied, which leads to feeling isolated; hide feelings of shame and inadequacy; themes of creativity and freedom.

Social Four	Shame

Highly sensitive; tend to blame self for deep feelings of unbelonging; present as shy or coy; feel shame when expressing desires and needs; intimate link with their own anguish.

Self-Preservation Five	Castle

Most withdrawn and boundaried; emotionally unexpressive; suspicious of extremes though they internally swing between minimalism and hoarding; present as guarded and distant.

Sexual Five (Countertype)	Confidence

Searching for deep connection; intense need for closeness; carefully hidden eccentricity; vibrant and sensitive inner landscape; attuned to rejection; avoid dependency on others.

Social Five	Totem

Balance the need for connection with need for boundaried seclusion; acuity to life's most important questions; find meaning by offering solutions; analytical problem solvers.

Self-Preservation Six	Warmth

Self-doubt leads to leaning on others for assurance; need safe place to vent concerns; earn stability by focusing on fears; affectionate and dependable to loved ones to self-protect.

Sexual Six (Countertype)	Strength

An asserting force confronting fears; present as stronger than they think they are; hide self-doubt; strong willed; rebelliously instigate movements against threats to security.

Social Six	Duty

Adhere to group convictions; find security in group association; defenders; incredibly high standards for sake of communal well-being; very loyal; strong sense of efficient duty.

Self-Preservation Seven   Keepers of the Castle

Form functional alliances to relieve restlessness; express freedom in lavishness and generosity; avoid being trapped by need for security; positive; continually active energy.

Sexual Seven   Fascination

Tending toward novelty and creativity; versatile and flexible; constantly exploring prospects of possibility; natural and optimistic dreamers; take relationships on gratifying adventures.

Social Seven (Countertype)   Sacrifice

Intentionally moderate drive for more into thoughtfulness toward others; repress exiting prospects for sake of commitments; long-term thinker; inspiring and creative.

Self-Preservation Eight   Survival

Resistant to invasions on their autonomy; powerful and direct; unintentionally intimidating; ensure all needs are met, which can present as selfish; fundamental need for gratification.

Sexual Eight   Possession

Largest force of energy; resistant to stifling attempts; entrench their dominance when provoked; impulsive; fiercely committed to inner circle; disconnected vulnerability.

Social Eight (Countertype)   Solidarity

Relaxed yet driven; highly motivated by service; channel aggression into socially concerned efforts; refrain from showing vulnerability; emphasis on relationships; promote goodness.

Self-Preservation Nine   Appetite

Focused on meeting basic needs; overfocused on preserving calm mentality; homebodies; lose themselves and fuse with relationships; tend to self-forget and self-deny life's gifts.

Sexual Nine	Union
Passively fuse with partner or friendship; preoccupation with their own sacrifices keep them from their interests, avoid being alone; relatable; confidant; tender and considerate.	

Social Nine (Countertype)	Participation
Driven to arbitrate harmony and social good; work hard for group's flourishing; merge with others; value cooperation above own sense of self; playful; inclusive; mediate divisions.	

[pages 253–267]

- Following Chris's example, "I identify as a Social dominant → Sexual supported → Self-Preservation repressed type Eight," write down your Instinct alignment with your type.

  _____

  _____

  _____

  _____

  _____

- In what way does your Subtype reveal more about how you relate to the world?

  _____

  _____

  _____

  _____

- What does your Subtype reveal about the way you relate to the Divine?

  _____

  _____

  _____

  _____

- Reflect on the last week. How often did you sense a compulsion to meet the needs of your dominant Instinct? How often are you aware of the needs of your repressed Instinct?

_____

_____

_____

_____

_____

_____

_____

- In what way does repressing your repressed Instinct hold you back from the whole of who you are? What distrust, discomfort, or dislike does it arise in you?

_____

_____

_____

_____

_____

_____

_____

While our back seat Instinct may never become the dominant driver in our unconscious, we can develop this Instinct. We *can* make deliberate efforts to bring it into awareness and practice greater governance of this back seat Instinct. [page 255]

- What human need does your repressed center ask for?

_____

_____

_____

_____

_____

_____

_____

- What gift does it offer you and the relational world you live in?

  _____

  _____

  _____

  _____

  _____

  _____

  _____

- What intentional efforts can you make to care for your repressed center?

  _____

  _____

  _____

  _____

  _____

  _____

  _____

- What feelings or thoughts of resistance in giving more care to your repressed center do you foresee yourself experiencing?

  _____

  _____

  _____

  _____

  _____

  _____

  _____

This introspective journey has led us along a pathway from our Heads, Hearts, and our Instincts, to face our deepest selves and continue to step into radical self-acceptance and compassionate belonging. [page 271] It's not easy or quick. But as we make our return to belonging with patience and intentionality, we'll discover that it is the most immensely life-giving and meaningful work.

- What would it mean for you to extend belonging to all Instincts?

  _____

  _____

  _____

  _____

  _____

  _____

- What would it mean for you to extend belonging to the process of your own inner evolution, the lifetime journey to compassionate self-acceptance?

  _____

  _____

  _____

  _____

  _____

  _____

- How might this journey to true belonging change the way you feel and think about yourself?

  _____

  _____

  _____

  _____

  _____

  _____

- How might the journey to true belonging shape the way you interact with those closest to you?

  _____

  _____

  _____

  _____

  _____

  _____

- How might this ongoing journey shape the way you show up to life and its opportunities?

_____

_____

_____

_____

_____

_____

REFLECTION OR DISCUSSION QUESTION

- Reflect on the story of the magic dragon in the concluding chapter of *The Enneagram of Belonging.* Answer the question Chris poses on page 275, "If a symbol of our unsophisticated purity is our inner child, or our deepest and realest selves, then why do we feel compelled to slay that dragon, or lose our innocence?" How might we continue the journey of befriending and connecting with our lost innocence? How might we serve as an encouraging force for those closest to us to do the same?

_____

_____

_____

_____

_____

_____

_____

Conclusion

Growing up doesn't mean leaving our Essence behind, but somehow, that is the very message each one of us internalized. We all came to believe that to be an adult, we had to diminish the potential of our inner child to become a mighty dragon—not a monster, but a messenger of truth and freedom.

But the truth our inner dragon has always told us, even when we've not listened, is that we are perfect just as we are. Every bit of ourselves belongs. Until every aspect of who we are belongs, including the parts we find the most offensive or least desirable, then no part of ourselves will truly belong. As we become aware of the parts of ourselves that need belonging, the Enneagram offers a road map for inner connection. More importantly, the Enneagram is a gentle reminder of who we've always, perfectly been all along. [page 276]

> "Radical compassion toward our self changes us. And when we are changed, the world is changed." [page 276]

The path of belonging is the journey of a lifetime. It is the sacred return to our original Essence. Indeed, the path of belonging requires patient, compassionate work. But the incredible truth is that as we make this journey ourselves, our example gives grace for others to do the same. It takes radical self-acceptance for us to live compassionately in the world, but it paves the way not only for inner belonging but also for the collective belonging of all humanity. [page 276]

Enneagram Consultations
and Workshops

Chris Heuertz is an Accredited Professional with the International Enneagram Association and an internationally recognized Enneagram teacher. Chris presents and consults internationally, introducing the Enneagram for personal and collective transformation with individuals, communities, universities, organizations, corporations, and small businesses.

To find an updated schedule for his Enneagram workshops, visit: www.sacredenneagram.org.

To schedule a one-on-one Enneagram consultation or a private or public workshop with Chris Heuertz, visit: http://gravitycenter.com/join/enneagram/.

Recommended Reading

Almaas, A. H. *Facets of Unity: The Enneagram of Holy Ideas*. Boston: Shambhala Publications, 1998.

Bakhtiar, Laleh. *The Sufi Enneagram: Sign of the Presence of God (Wajhullah): The Secrets of the Symbol Unveiled*. Chicago: Institute of Traditional Psychology, 2013.

Calhoun, Adele, Doug Calhoun, Clare Loughrige, and Scott Loughrige. *Spiritual Rhythms for the Enneagram: A Handbook for Harmony and Transformation*. Downers Grove, IL: InterVarsity Press, 2019.

Chestnut, Beatrice. *The Complete Enneagram: 27 Paths to Greater Self-Knowledge*. Berkeley, CA: She Writes Press, 2013.

Fernández Christlieb, Fátima. *Where on Earth Did the Enneagram Come From?* Ciudad de México: Editorial Pax México, 2016.

Goldberg, Michael J. *The Nine Ways of Working: How to Use the Enneagram to Discover Your Natural Strengths and Work More Effectively*. Philadelphia, PA: Da Capo Press, a member of the Perseus Book Group, 1999.

Heuertz, Christopher L. *The Sacred Enneagram: Finding Your Unique Path to Spiritual Growth*. Grand Rapids, MI: Zondervan, 2017.

Heuertz, Christopher L. with Estee Zandee. *The Sacred Enneagram Workbook: Finding Your Unique Path to Spiritual Growth*. Grand Rapids, MI: Zondervan, 2019.

Ichazo, Óscar. *Between Metaphysics and Protoanalysis: A Theory for Analyzing the Human Psyche*. New York: Arica Institute Press, 1982.

Lapid-Bogda, Ginger. *The Art of Typing: Powerful Tools for Enneagram Typing*. Santa Monica, CA: The Enneagram in Business Press, 2018.

Maitri, Sandra. *The Enneagram of Passions and Virtues: Finding the Way Home*. New York: Penguin, 2005.

————. *The Spiritual Dimension of the Enneagram.* New York: Penguin Putnam, 2000.

Naranjo, Claudio. *Character and Neurosis: An Integrative View.* Nevada City, CA: Gateways/ IDHHB Publishers, 1994.

Palmer, Helen. *The Enneagram: Understanding Yourself and the Others in Your Life.* New York: HarperOne, 1988.

Riso, Don Richard, and Russ Hudson. *The Wisdom of the Enneagram: The Complete Guide to Psychological and Spiritual Growth for the Nine Personality Types.* New York: Bantam, 1999.

Rohr, Richard, and Andreas Ebert. *The Enneagram: A Christian Perspective.* Translated by Peter Heinegg. New York: Crossroad, 2006.

Schafer, William M. *Roaming Free Inside the Cage: A Daoist Approach to the Enneagram.* Bloomington, IN: iUniverse, 2009.

Wagner, Jerome. *Nine Lenses on the World: The Enneagram Perspective.* Evanston, IL: Enneagram Studies and Applications, 2010.

NINE

The Enneagram
Documentary

For more info:

enneagram.movie

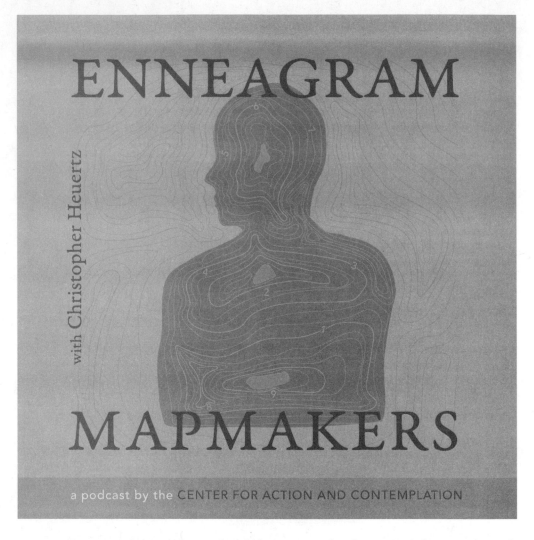

ENNEAGRAM
with Christopher Heuertz
MAPMAKERS
a podcast by the CENTER FOR ACTION AND CONTEMPLATION

ENNEAGRAM MAPMAKERS explores the interior landscapes of the ego through conversations with legacy teachers such as Richard Rohr, Helen Palmer, and Russ Hudson. Hosted by Christopher Heuertz, author of *The Sacred Enneagram* and *The Enneagram of Belonging*, this podcast journeys to the origins of an ancient and often misunderstood system designed to help us live a more embodied and integrated life. Transcend the temptation to fixate on a specific number and discover how to embrace all types within you.